Joshua Barnes

Gerania

A New Discovery of a Little Sort of People

Joshua Barnes

Gerania
A New Discovery of a Little Sort of People

ISBN/EAN: 9783337258092

Printed in Europe, USA, Canada, Australia, Japan

Cover: Foto ©Suzi / pixelio.de

More available books at **www.hansebooks.com**

GERANIA:

A NEW
DISCOVERY
OF A
Little sort of PEOPLE

Anciently Discoursed of, called

PYGMIES.

With a lively Description

Of their Stature, Habit, Manners, Buildings, Knowledge, and Government, being very delightful and profitable.

By *JOSHUA BARNES,*
of *Emanuel College, Cambridge.*

Ingentes animos angusto in Corpore versant. Virg.

Ἴδμεν ψεύδεα πολλὰ λέγειν ἐτύμοισιν ὁμοῖα. Hesiod.

LONDON,
Printed by *W. G.* for *Obadiah Blagrave,*
at the Sign of the *Printing-press,* over against the *Pump* in *Little-Britain,* 1675.

THE

PREFACE

TO THE

READER.

There is such an innate
principle in the Hearts
of most Men, that they
are able to admit nothing for
currant, but what is obvious,
nor reckon any thing credible,
unless it be visible : But seeing
almost every Climate doth pecu-
liarly afford something rare and
unnsual, it stands with reason,
that some Climate should in

especial

especial manner produce some
more extraordinary Novelty, if
not to others incredible, yet at
least wonderful, and not easily
digested for a truth.

That there is a Nation of Men,
called Pygmies, hath been a-
verred by Authors of pregnant
Ingenuity, solid Judgement,
and authentick Esteem; and
though many have omitted a due
inquest into this matter, yet such
and so many have given their
suffrages for the certainty of it,
that we may without the impu-
tation of credulity account it no
fable. And why should it be
thought improbable, that Nature
(who continually delights to
embroider

embroider *this Frame of Being*, *with variety of Creatures*) *should somewhere produce Men of a smaller Character than our selves, considering those Capital Letters* (*Gyants I mean*) *have been known so far to exceed us on the other side?* That *it is not unbefitting the way of natural Productions, we may quickly ascertain our minds, if we do but reflect on those many* Pumilio's *and* Tom-thumb's, *which even among People of the largest size are frequently exhibited as Examples of the other Copies. But having only given an occasion here for others to exercise their ratiocination, I shall content*

tent my self with this concise preamble, as satisfactory enough to the Judicious, who indeed may better perswade themselves by more important reasons, which their own due consideration may suggest unto them, and so begin my intended Discourse, if not altogether true, yet not wholly vain, nor perhaps deficient, in what may exhilerate a Witty Fancy, or inform a bad Moralist.

GERA-

GERANIA:

OR,

NEWS

FROM THE

PYGMIES.

ON the Seventh of *November*, failing as pleasantly on the *Ganges* as the natural impetuosity of that Stream would permit, the Weather changing on a suddain, our Ship Veer'd about to the Larboard, and we were driven by a violent cold and dry North wind, into a narrow Arm of a great Lake on the utmost Borders of *India*;

B   that

that takes its rife from one common head with that famous River; there having escaped that direful embrace, which the inhofpitable Waves had feem'd to profer us, we proceeded fo flowly, as if a *Remora* had held our Keel, or rather as if we had caft Anchor in the *Mare Mortuum*; but having at laft with much labour conquer'd Three Leagues towards the neareft Land, in about eight and twenty hours, we began to eafe our felves, by defifting from our toyl, and by a general participation of the refidue of our Victuals, which as yet held out as we defired. After this refrefhment, the golden Rayes of *Phaethon* began to make the Eaftern Mountains blufh, that all their coftly Stones and glittering Sands, were not fufficiently rich and auguft, to welcome fo illuftrious a Monarch; and the gentle Breezes

of

of the Lake having on the Shoar
faluted the delicious fannings of
Aurora, return'd to us in foft
whifperings, and affured us of the
arrival of that Rofie-fingred Queen.
At this, I and two of my Friends
advanced our felves on the Deck,
and at the fame time the glorious
Prince of Day feem'd to add fpeed
to his fiery Horfes, and return our
Complement in a nearer approach
to us. But how foon were our
thoughts divided betwixt fear and
admiration; while the Mountains,
which but now appeared to us as
flaming, began to confefs themfelves of that more innocent and
amiable Luftre, which attends the
brighteft of Metals, when it is bur-
nifhed moft furprizingly? We ga-
zed fomething earneftly at this
amazing fpectacle, and propofing
to our hopes no lefs than Golden
Mountains, we ftill fixing our

Eyes on that defireable object, 'till
a fuddain noife of the rufling of
Leaves alarum'd our Ears, which
kept fentinel at the fide portals of
our Brain, and they recalling our
Eyes from their ftudious curiofity,
fent them towards the Shoar, as He-
ralds, to enquire the reafon of that
fo eafie difturbance.   Where we
beheld a few Perfons, whom we
thought Men, Inhabitants of that
place; though they fent no Voices
to frighten or invite us, but only
certain mimical and ridiculous
Geftures, from whence notwith-
ftanding, we might foon collect,
that they profefs'd us no ill-will.
With which encouraged, we re-
doubled our endeavours to reach the
Land, and a ftedfaft blaft or two
backing our defign, that in lefs
than an hour we touch'd the Shoar,
where we might eafily difcern, that
our Invitants forbore to welcome us
with

with acclamations, or with obliging words, to complement us to a
nearer acceſs , not becauſe they
lack'd Civility , but wanted thoſe
channels of Expreſſion, which we
call Mouths. Their Poſture, though
ſomething uncouth , was not ſo
rude, but that it declared them to
be ſo far different from Brutes, that
nothing ſeem'd abſent , which
might make them compleat Men ,
but the Gentleman-Uſher of all
Knowledge, *Sermocination*. On
their Heads they proudly wore
green Boughs, the wanton Leaves
whereof, ſeem'd deſirous to ſhow
themſelves by their ſoft whiſpering,
more Vocal than their Bearers.
Their Habit was of the woolly
Moſs of Trees, moſt artificially
cemented with Gum, and inter-
ſperſed with delectable Poſies; a-
bout their Necks they wore pleaſant chains of odoriferous Flowers,

the smell whereof is their chiefest
aliment, except that of a certain
lushious and nourishing Juice,
which they suck thorough a small
Tube or Pipe, into that little Ori-
fice, which Nature hath granted
them in the place and stead of
Mouths. Their Legs are destitute
of any other covering, but what
their natural Hair supplies them
with; but the Nails of both Hands
and Feet were augmented to such a
length, by their Sylvan Diet and
Ignorance of more humane ways,
that they served them instead of
Weapons, against the strongest
wild Beast, who was alwayes too
weak for them; and with those
they dug up Flowers and Plants,
as they pleased. They received us
with no vulgar Civility, expressing by their nodds and loquacious
motions of their active Limbs, no
small pride at our presence. But
poor

poor Creatures! Alaſs, our ſtock of Victuals was but low, and we were not ſo good Chamæleons as they, to live upon Air; neither could their fragrant Chapplets prevent our Famiſhment, if we ſtaid longer there. Wherefore being ſoon weary of their dumb converſation, we reſolved in time, to ſeek ſome other People, whoſe liberality might ſtore us with Proviſion for another Voyage, and whoſe community of living, being not ſo abhorrent from ours, might make them more ſenſible of our neceſſities, and ſo more prone to relieve them. To which end, having left twenty Men in the Ship, and all the remaining Victuals, (which was enough to laſt them five or ſix days) and ſolemnly promiſing not to go far, but to find out ſome place, and return again within ſix or ſeven days; after Breakfaſt, on *Monday*

Morning

Morning, and Prayers for the Divine protection and direction, all the reſt of our Company (which was thirty five) being directed by the ſigns of the *Aſtomi* (for ſo theſe People are called) went ſtraight up towards the Mountains.   It was now ſpring time of the Year, yet notwithſtanding the warmth of the Seaſon, the Mountains were cloathed with a double Garment, the embroidered Veſt of *Flora*, and the Eye-dazling Mantle of *Phæbus*, and while they glittered in their eminence and apparel, the æmulous Valleys raiſed their ſwelling breaſts of Corn to ſuch an exuberance of height, as if they intended to make the Mountains acknowledge themſelves inferiour to them : Which lovely contention , was ſuch an incentive to the Poetical Genius of one in our Company, that he could not forbear exonerating his Fancy in this Gratulatory manner.   I.

I.

Where are We, Muses? Only you
Can tell this lovely place;
Where Flora *doth her youth renew,*
And adds each day new lustre to her face.

II.

Is this fair Tempe? *Or the Clime*
Where you with Graces dwell;
For Ceres *here is in her prime,*
And Bacchus *joy doth in each clustre swell?*

III.

Is it Elizium? *No, oh! no!*
For here Sol *shows his rays;*
And Fruits and Flowers for Men do grow;
Souls in Elizium *live not by such ways.*

IV.

What ever place 'tis call'd, thrice blest
Are those that here do live:
But Nature sure, spares in the rest,
When she these blessings doth so freely give.

And

And truly the laſt Diſtick was
Prophetical enough , for though
theſe Bleſſings are ſo ſuperabun-
dantly great , yet thoſe who have
the fruition of them, are Microcoſ-
mically little to ſuch a degree , that
I verily believe , excepting ſome
other parts of their own Nation ,
they are the ſmalleſt People in the
whole Habitable.   The firſt we
met with were ſome Children ,
driving an Herd of Kids ; we pre-
ſently began to admire with our
ſelves at the Ingenuity of the Inhabitants , thinking they had invented theſe little Engins , ſo as by
Clock-work to make them walk :
But we were ſoon put out of that
fondneſs , when the little Imps beholding our Gigantick ſize , run
away ſhrieking , and the nimble
Kids , run ſcatter'd back in no leſs
confuſion than their drivers ; truly
a ſmall matter would have made

us

us run away too, we were fo a-
maz'd at fuch an intricate accident.
Some thought it was the Land of
the *Faries* , and implored me to
lead them back ; others fuppofing
them Devils , exhorted me to re-
cal my foot-fteps , and haft back a-
gain, while there was opportunity.
But Hunger was a more prevalent
Oratour at that time ; for we had
now Travail'd hard two dayes and
an half, having only broke our
faft the Morning we fet out, and
fince not met with any thing to
allay our Appetite, except fome few
ftrange Fruits we found in the
way ; fo that if we went back,
we were fure to faint and famifh a-
mong fruitlefs Flowers, and unpro-
fitable Dainties ; wherefore I encouraged them to proceed cheerfully, and rather to venture any death
than kill themfelves by Fear, and
dye by Famine. But they had had
little

little stomach to follow my advice,
if the Poet *Eucompsus* had not assisted me with his Oration; and indeed he was our only support and
solace in Travail , being a very
merry Fellow, eminently ingenious,
of a large and noble Soul , and my
singular good Friend. But because
you may better conjecture at his
Person by his speech , and that I
may do him right , I'le give you
his very Words, as near as I can
remember; which for the future,
as oft as occasion serves , I will
promise you to do , whether they
be Verse or Prose; because I ever
took good heed of his Discourses
and other Fancies. And thus he
began : *Friends and Companions , let
me desire you for two or three Minutes
only, to compose your selves , for I have
something to say, that will please and
secure you.* At this they all came
about him, and stood quaking , to
hear

hear what he would deliver, like a
timorous Herd of Deer, when
they are firſt terrifi'd with the approaching noiſe of Huntſmen and
Dogs. And though I could not
deviſe what his intent might be, I
doubted not, but it would be very
convenient for the occaſion; but
thus he went on: *It is not the manner of gracious Heaven to place unbe-
coming Inhabitants in ſo happy a Soil;
nor can any Man of reaſon or judg-
ment believe theſe Creatures to be
Faries (i. e. nothing) or any ſpiritual
Being. In ſhort, they are Men*; (here
they ſtared at him monſtrouſly,)
*I, Men, I ſay, rational as we are, and
I doubt, far more couragious; for did
you not obſerve them ſometimes to make
a ſtand, and looking at us, ſeem'd almoſt
prepared to come to us? And certain-
ly, though the unuſual largeneſs of our
Bulk might juſtly amaze them, had we
had their hearts, we ſhould not have
trembled*

trembled so easily at the sight of such minute Animals. I have often heard of Pygmies, that they ride on Goats, and those Kids we saw are Colts, proportionable enough to such Coursers. The darkness of their Complexion being a consequence of this Climate, why should we suspect any Diabolical Apparition? Seeing Devils, as Spirits, can have no colour at all, because such Qualities are only proper to Bodies; and if no colour, why may they not in the assumption of Bodies to them, invest that Body they assume with any other colour as well as Black? For thus, though we paint Devils of that colour, which is most different from ours; so the Æthiopians are accustomed to paint them white, and perhaps with no less absurdity. Having therefore shown them to be no immaterial Substances, it remains, they must be material, that is (as may be gathered from their self-motion and Voice) Animal Creatures;
and

and their shrieking being much after the manner of our Children, though more sharp and squeaking, as well as their shape and habit perswades us they must be Men. Then let us view them, *their manner of Government, their Buildings, Customs and Labours; which will prove no doubt the most delectable adventure, that all our Travails did ever yet present us with.* You would not think of what wondrous efficacy thefe few words were, being confidently uttered by one, whom they all knew to be well Learned in Geography; and of great Eloquence, which was attended with a fecret energy, called *Peitho,* which made him perfwade the moft obftinate, and lead his hearers by their Ears, as Bears are led by their Nofes. But yet there was one obftacle more, by reafon of one unreafonable Fellow, called *Pan-derfon,* a *Romanift,* who began to
exclaim

exclaim after this foolish manner. *Oh ye Mad-men! to follow a whimsical Poet to this Land of Misery; though such kind of Men are not only believed to go to Hell themselves, but are known to lead others thither. This place is the Gate of Hell, those are Devils, which he would fain perswade us to be men; and the Kids and Goats, that he confesses abound there, we are told by Scripture, are the Damned, which those Devils are driving to some place of Torment; nor is it strange, that the place seems so pleasant and delectable, for they say, the way to Hell is strewed with Roses. And I fear, if you proceed, (for I am resolved not to follow) that these Mountains will indeed prove flaming ones, as they seem'd at first; a just punishment for your temerity.* And saying this, he hasted backward, fumbling with his Beads, and Crossing himself all over, continually flinging

Ora

Ora-pro-nobis'es to the Virgin *Mary.*
Which when *Eucompsus* perceived,
he holp to Crofs him too, and fell
into fuch a violent Laughter, that
while none of us could refrain,
the noife being at leaft trebly in-
creafed by the reverberation of that
mountainous and hilly Country,
put *Pandeifon* into fuch a fright,
that he haftned down the Mountains, like one poffeffed, till his
præcipitant fear gave him fuch a
fall, that we thought he had broke
his Neck; yet for all this, our
Laughter was rather augmented
than diminifhed, till a charitable
Thought for our Companion, enforced us to a reftraint. And this
Mirth did us fo much good, as to
make us forget our Hunger, which
we could hardly elfe have tolerated
longer. So we fent four of our
Servants to bring him back to us,
who made a very fpeedy return
C   again

again with poor *Pandeison* in a
swound, his Cloaths and Face all
torn, and his left Arm broken;
all which, seem'd to us a very cheap
ransom for his Neck. But as soon
as ever he recover'd, he winked
very slighly, and of a suddain
cry'd out on us, as if we were
Devils too, which occasioned us
to Laugh once more. But at last,
finding how still and harmless we
bore our selves, he took the confi-
dence to open his Eyes a little
wider, and having come to the
knowledge of us, he intreated
our pardon, and desired, we would
not leave him behind us, but carry
him to the next House we should
see, and rest there till he was re-
covered. Then we cut up some
Grafs and Flowers, and having
spred them on a Bed, which we
had composed of Twigs and Boughs
we committed him to our four Servants,

vants, to be laid thereon, and fo
to be brought after us. Thus all
was at rights again. The firft
Province we came to, was that of
Gadozolia, the People whereof
being called *Gadozim*, are the
faireft, largeft, and moft ftately
of all other *Pygmies*. The very
fight of the Smoak here gave heat
to our refolutions, and we made
fuch haft, being enforced by Hunger, that to ufe a Scholaftick
Phrafe, We did even devour the
way. At laft being directed by
a great Smoak, which was fufficiently obfervable in fo thin and
ferene an Air, we arrived before
a ftately Fabrick of about 200
Foot fquare, yet not above fixty
Foot high, made all of well-carved
Wood, which abounds in that
Country, called *Geranophonon*; a
Wood, that contrary to the nature
of all other, dyes when it is in the

Earth,

Earth, after it hath grown twenty Years; but when it is fell'd down, it proves ftronger, and looks more veget than before; fo that age, which conquers all other things, makes this to triumph; and Worms themfelves, as knowing their attempt will prove vain, never corrode, or fo much as come near it. On the Battlements of this Caftle, (for a Caftle it proved) was Earth fpread, fo that we took it for arable Ground, and Corn was befprinkled in the counterfeit Furrows; at each corner of which were Stakes faftned, and four Nets fo artificially fpread, that no fooner could any thing of weight touch that ground, which is called *Geodyctyum*, but the Nets are clofed on all fides, and the Prey that is taken, lyes hampered on the *Geodyctyum.* We needed not to crave entrance at this Caftle, for before we came to the Gates, there met

nine young dandiprat-Gal-
bout two Foot and an half
: Foot high, attired in a
loured Silk, with Tur-
their Heads of Linnen,
over with cloth of Gold,
ned with divers fplendent
about their Back was caft
of blew Sarcinet, which
ered upon the right Shoul-
a golden Button, over
ere was caft a fmall chain
:, whereon a rich Sword
a Foot long was hung,
gs were cover'd with fine
and on their Feet they
ndals of Sheeps Leather,
e beftriding a lufty Ram,
lded Horns, and Trappings
ith fparkling Diamonds.
had by this time pretty
firmed us all in the opinion,
fe were *Pygmies*; fo that
not much admire at the
C 3   ftrange

strange Equipage of such dwarfish
Orlando's , but bowing our Bodies
to them, stood still in a posture to
receive them , when three of the
formost, and as it appeared , most
Noble of them, turning back, and
making their followers to stand ,
of a suddain , sprung , as it were ,
with one consent , from their Ram-
Horses , and with admirable cele-
rity coming up to us , first boldly
beheld our Faces , and then in the
Indian Language bad us all welcome to their Countrey. *Encompsus*
and my self, and another Friend of
ours, having formerly for some years
Traffick'd in the *Indies* , made
shift to understand them , and to
return them an assurance, that we
came in peace , and desired only to
Sojourn so long in their Country,
as to repair our lack of Provision ,
and by observing their Customs to
encrease our Knowledge. They
having

having affured us of all that might
conduce to our fatisfaction , entrea-
ted us to follow them , pointing
to the Caftle , which they called
the Royal Bulwark : Then they
nimbly remounted , and placing
themfelves before our company ,
two others on each fide , and the
remaining two behind; in this order we all moved towards the Royal
Bulwark , they riding foftly with
us. But when we came to the
Gates , one of their Company took
from his Neck a fmall Rams-horn,
tipt with Silver, and ty'd with a
Silken Cord , and having blown
three blafts with fuch ftrength, that
he was forced to ftagger in his Saddle , the Caftle-gates were immediately opened by twenty Men, who
pull'd them wide by filken Cords,
which were faftned to the Gates
with Silver Rings.   And they di-
viding themfelves on each fide the

C 4   folding

folding Doors, ftood ftill, affording
us a large paffage, when the three
Chiefs, that went before us, aligh-
ting, gave their Steeds to their Servants to put them up, and walked
ftreight before us into a fpacious
Hall, where was an Ancient Gentleman about three Foot and an half
high, with a Coronet of Gold,
befet with precious ftones, and a
long Robe of flowered Satin, all
be-laced wiah Spangles, who
ftood leaning on a ftaff to bid us
welcome. The three *Heroes* ran to
meet him, and having fell on their
Knees, pointed back to us, and faid
fomething, as we thought, on our
behalf; when having raifed them
up, he walked forward, as well as
his age would permit him, to meet
us : We were now all entred into
the Hall when he came to us, and
having yielded him as profound
refpect as was poffible, he re-falu-
ted

ted us, and making figns that we fhould move forward, prefently thofe twenty Men, who had opened the Gates, came in loaded with Velvet-Cufhions, two of them to each Cufhion, and placing their burthen decently on each fide of a very fmall, but ftately Chair, they brought in two Courfes of Cufhions more, which made thirty in number, as many as our company were, befides the four Servants and *Pandiefon*, whom now we could no where fpye. At this time the Sun began to decline his golden head, and feeble Day feem'd ready to faint under the burthen of twelve hours, when an hundred young Virgins, cloathed all in white Sarcenet, entered the Hall with burning Tapers in their Hands, which they placed in Golden Sockets, that were made on the fides of the Hall, and fo retired with

a

a folemn filence. And here I be-
-gan to think nothing wanting
to a complete entertainment, but
a good Supper, and my Stomach
being fomthing importunate, while
the looks of our Company put me
in mind of their neceffities, I
could no longer forbear, but rifing
from my Cufhion, came before
the Ancient Gentleman, who was
now ready to fit in his Chair of
State, and firft bowing my Body
three times, (a fafhion which I ob-
ferved in them) I unfolded our
condition to him in the *Indian* Language to this purpofe; *Great Ruler*,
(*Eucompfus* fmiled at that Epithet)
*of the Bulwark Royal, we all eafily
perceive, that our Treatment here
is as Noble and Magnificent as the
higheft ambition could defire; but our
hungery Stomachs put us in mind to fa-
tisfie them before the Eyes, that being
a work more neceffary for Nature, and*
help-

helpful for all other operations: — I was going to proceed, when he smilingly interrupted me, and told me, he knew all this before, having read in our Countenances, that we wanted both Food and Sleep; and therefore, he said, he intended not to trouble us with any Difcourfe or inquiries that Night, but only to take care, that after a good treatment, (which would be brought up prefently) we fhould be conducted to our feveral rooms, and there left to our repofe. For he faid, about two or three hours before, fome Children of his Chief Goat-herds, had given him information of our arrival; and that though they had never feen fuch tall Men before, yet he had been long acquainted with Men as big as we, having frequently entertain'd Embaffadours from the *Macrobians*, a People of the fame *India*; and having himfelf,

with

with his three Sons, gon on several Embassies to the neighbour Nations. While he was making this brief relation, the 20 Men brought into the Hall store of Goats-Milk, in Silver Dishes, each whereof was born by a couple of them, both for state, and perhaps because they were too heavy for one of them to bear, and fetching two Courses more, till we had a Dish for every one, they softly retreated; after which a couple of Gentlewomen brought in the Spoons, made of a certain bright Shell, and after that, ten of those twenty Men came in, every one with a fine wrought Basket on his Head, wherein were three Cakes, about the bigness of a six peny Loaf, though not so thick, made of purer Flower, than any part of *Europe* yields, and so fragrant with Spices, that the greatest Monarch in the

Earth

Earth would not defire a finer Manchet; and laftly, there was fet before each of us a Bowl of pleafant and wholfome Wine, called by them *Zythus*, made of the Vine *Perfephonodia*, which *Zagreus* planted there before the Birth of *Bacchus*; a Wine more like Nectar, than any drink of Mortals. We were going to fall on what was fet before us, when the fuddain noife of a golden Bell made us forbear, and look out, till a tall, flender, and comely Perfonage appeared in a Robe of pureft white, conftellated with the figure of the Celeftial Bodies, and on his Fore-head this mark ✚ in a golden Meddal; who taking up a Cake of Bread, and ftanding on an Ivory ftep, fpoke thus in *Englifh*; *O Thou, who though never fully comprehended, art fignified to weak Mortals by the fign which I thy Servant continually bear on my*

Fore-

Forehead, whom our Nation adores
and magnifies above all powers, showre
down thine heavenly Benediction on
these thy Creatures, and hear this
Prayer of mine, for thy Compassions
sake, in the behalf of these Strangers,
who come from a place, where thy Salvation is known, that they may recover strength thereby and refreshment
from their Travail; Grant this, O thou,
who wast a stranger in Ægypt, and a
Sojourner in Bethlehem, for thine
own most meritorious sake: So be it.
While he was saying this, he ex-
pressed so much fervency, that it
struck us with a devout veneration
and respect of his person; nor did
it a little amaze us to hear him use
our Language with such freedom,
as if he had been an *English* Native;
but his suddain leaving us, gave us
opportunity of eating our Suppers,
which we did with good Stomachs,
till the first brunt of our Hunger
was

was fatiated, and we began to feed
more leifurely, which afforded us
time to feed our Eyes too with the
Splendour of our entertainment,
and the rarities of the Hall; which
was all hung with rich Arras,
whereon was pourtrayed the Story
of *Phryxus* the Son of *Athamas*,
here he fwam over the yet un-nam'd
River on the golden back of the
Ram, and here the timorous Girl be-
fallen off, still ftrugling with
thofe Waves, which her death
has made fo famous; and now the
Hellefpont, as feeming content
with fo great a Sacrifice, fmooth'd
its frothy cheeks in calmnefs. On
an other fide was a lively defcrip-
tion of the Fight of *Damafen* (an
Earth-bore Gyant) with the Dragon. How young *Tylus* walking
by the banks of the River *Hermus*,
chanc'd to touch with his Hand a
fleeping Dragon, being ignorant
what

what it was, but the incenfed
Creature bending back his Neck,
and opening his impartial Jaws,
ran againft him, and lafhing his
fides, fhook the Tempeftuous burthen of his fatal Tail, which he
caft about his Neck in undiffolva-
ble Spires, ftill fending from his
poifonous Throat the frothy mef-
fengers of indubitable death : This
was the only chain which grim
Lachefis allotted the youth, though
glorious with dazling Scales, yet
moft pernicious to the wearers of
it; and in the embrace of this,
like a fweet Flower covered with
Dew, he bow'd to the Earth, and
left the Nymph his Sifter, to mourn
his untimely fate : She forgat not
a pious Groan or two, and then
went in fearch of the Dragon, to
know how big he was; for it was
not one Travailer, nor one She-
pherd he had deftroyed, nor was

Tylus

Tylus alone flain by him, nor did he only feed on Beafts while he lay basking in the Wood, but often tearing up a ftrong Tree with his Teeth, he would fwallow it, and often drawing back a Travailer with the very force of his magnetick Breath, he had been feen afar off to receive an whole Man in his gaping Throat. The Nymph *Meroe* faw from far this Mutherer of her Brother, and was fhaken with horrour, to behold the thick rows of his peftiferous Teeth, and the Crown of Death circumfcribed in the limits of his wide Throat. And making fad lamentation in the Wood, fhe met *Damafen*, the huge Son of Earth, whom contention had nurs'd up, and *Lucina* her felf had arm'd; an Infant, yet terrible; a Suckling, yet Warlike, and a Child of more than humane ftrength: Him the

D Nymph

Nymph beholding near a side of the Wood, fell on her Knees, and sobbing mournfully, show'd him the Monstrously-crawling Murtherer of her Brother; and poor *Tylus* yet strugling with death in the dust. The Gyant gladly undertook her quarrel, and wrenching up a huge Tree from his Mother Earth, he presently came before the cruel Dragon, who had by this time sounded the trumpet of his horrid Hissing to the Battle. Never were two such Monsters met together, the one covering near fifty Acres with his Scaly folds, the other threatning the Stars with his lofty front; the fearful Dragon had soon ty'd the Legs of *Damasen* with a double Sphincter, and opening the gates of his Teeth, with an enraged look, that breathed death, he darted at him the moist weapons of Poison from his Lips, and

and leap'd up towards his Head:
But the proud *Damafen* fcorning
fuch familiarity with a Beaft, eafily
repell'd him with his Hand, and
fmiting him with the Oak on his
Temples, he rooted the Tree once
more, fending it and death together into the Monfter; who folding
himfelf up in clofe wreaths,
lay dead on the Earth; when of
a fuddain the Female Dragon coming by, as it were on purpofe, faw
her dead Male, and prefently ha-
fted to the herbiferous Mountain,
whence cropping with her vipe-
rous Teeth the Flower of *Jove*,
fhe brought back the Medicinal
Herb in her Lips, and prefently
apply'd it to the dry Chaps of the
dead Serpent; the hinder part of
him was now livelefs, the formoft
moved, and lovingly joyn'd it felf
to the other part, which now
recover'd motion too; thus having

D 2　　　　drawn

drawn his returned Breath through his cold Mouth, he soon after began to open his Throat and send forth accustomed Hisses, and so returned with his loving Mate to his secret Den. And then fair *Meroe*, who beheld all this, took up the Flower of *Jove*, and applyed it to the Mouth and Nostrils of her breathless Brother; but the vital Herb with its Virtual leaves, re-insouled the Body, and forced his departed Spirit to return again, infusing heat and life through every part: At this Young *Tylus* rose again, like a Man who after his nocturnal Sleep shakes off the Eye-binding shackles of lazy *Somnus*, and leaps from his Bed on his vigourous Feet; again, his late congealed Blood began to run its wonted circulation through the channels of the Veins, and his newly released Hands began to actuate, his
Face

Face was reinvefted with its former Beauty, and ftrength returned to his Body, light to his Eyes, and fpeech to his Lips.   On an other fide was pourtrayed the contention of emulous *Arachne* with the Goddefs *Minerva*; but the moft admirable rarity there was the Spiders Web, which was made by Metamorphofed *Arachne* ; never were threads fo fmall, fo artificially wrought by any humane Hand before.   Thefe reprefentations and more were expreffed to the life on thofe ingenious Hangings, which while we curioufly run over, our Stomachs had remitted much of their former rapacity, and we had leifure to ruminate on the wonderful and undeferved Civilities we had received from fo fmall a Nation, not only fometimes remembring the goodnefs of their Bread and Wine, but often

re-

reflecting on that admirable skill
had been shown in the Work on
the Arras; at which time we,
seeming not to employ all our Or-
gans at Supper, were supprized
with such an Harmonious Consort
of Musick , that every Sense
seem'd converted into that of
Hearing , and our Apostate Appetite, to prefer this Auditory
Banquet.   Which so inflam'd the
Aery Soul of *Encompsus*, that being very dexterous in that faculty,
he warbled out *extempore* this rapture
with a most sweet and low Voice
to the *Indian* Tune, which was
then play'd.

I.

What sound is this, that captivates mine ears,
    Inthrals my Sense, and wings my Soul?
Jove sure, if he this Consort hears ,
    Stands listning from the starry Pole ,
Contemning all the Musick of his Sphears ,
Though mixt with Ganymed's nectarean bowl.

II.

II.

Such Numbers did from the Orphæan *Lyre*
Enliven quick-ear'd Trees, and move
In decent Dance, (if Fame's no lyar)
The whole admiring Thracian *Grove,*
So Phæbus *did with* Mercury *conspire,*
When Peleus *wedded his* Nereian *Love.*

III.

Such Numbers from the skill'd Amphion *fell,*
When stones kept measure to his sound,
When temper'd Air could work so well,
And potent Verse so strong was found;
It made rough Quarries by the quavering spell
Jump in Symetrick *Piles the City round.*

IV.

But since(wise Nature*)thou hast freely made*
So small a Race so great a Quire,
Since they our priviledge invade,
And mount as high as we or higher
In thy great Secrets: hence small things be said
The fittest things to Love, and to admire.

And

And here the Musick ending, his Pegasean heat was a little cooled, when the youngest of the Three Heroes (who the Ancient Gentleman before called his Sons) stept behind *Eucompsus*, and having obligingly commended his Voice, he thank'd him for the Honour conferr'd on their Solemnity, and confessing that by a familiarity with his Country Priests, he had attained to so much knowledge at left in the *English* Tongue, as might make him perceive the drift of his Song to be in praise of that Consort, he therefore desired to be permitted to make his return in the like nature ; which *Eucompsus* gladly condescended to, and whispered to me and my Friend his intent, so that we were almost Ear-starved with expectation of that genial entertainment; when of a suddain, the Musick having

play'd

the PYGMIES. 41

of the young Heroe was fo ra-
vifhingly elevated , that foaring
above the ufual pitch of meaner
Poets , he warbled forth, with the
moft gratioufly furprizing Voice
imaginable , this Song in the *Indian*
Language.

I.

'Tis not our Mufick (Strangers brave)
That can your Senfes bind;
Our Verfes no fuch Magick have
Your Generous Spirits to enflave:
Alas ! You're too too kind.

II.

Yet from the heat of Phœbus rayes
We're not fo far remov'd,
But that we fometimes purchafe Bayes,
And wander through thofe flow'ry wayes,
So much by Mufes lov'd.

III.

But since the Sacred Treble-three
  Now in this Castle dwell;
(For you have brought them here we see)
We hope our Canto's may agree
  Some other time as well.

IV.

But now, fair Nox, that dost attire
  Thy self in Sable Vest;
Be thou propitious, we desire,
While these kind Strangers do retire,
  And sweetly take their Rest.

After this favourable *Vale*, the residue of our Supper was taken away, in the same order it was all brought in, and immediately, upon the ringing of the Golden Bell, the Priest, which they call a *Dramesco* (*i. e.* a representative of Christ) returned in the same Habit and

and manner as before, who moun-
ting on the aforementioned Ivory
Bafis, returned the Thanks of the
Guefts to the Supream Deity in
thefe words, *O thou ineffable Being,
whofe Goodnefs is as boundlefs as thine
Empire, in the name of thefe Strangers, I thine unworthy Subftitute,
return thee deferved Thanks for this
prefent comfortable repaft, as well as
thy daily favours to them; befeeching
thee, that as their weak Bodies,
through thy Mercy, are nourifhed with
daily Food, fo their immortal Souls
may continually be fatisfied with the
Spiritual Banquets of thy Grace, that
both their Souls and Bodies may joyn
in a pure Life, to the Glory of thy
Great Name, and the Health of their
own Souls: Grant this of thine un-
fpeakeable Clemency. So be it.*

Having fo faid, he bleffed us,
and bad us reft in Peace; adding,
that he would fee us the next
mor-

morning, and confer with us; at
which saying, we all rose up and
bow'd to him, which he seem'd to
take no notice of, but went directly out of the Hall; after which
there came in four Damsels (who
were of the hundred fore-mentio-
ned) with lighted Tapers in their
hands, who approaching to me
first, as being the Chief, beck'ned
to me to follow them, which I did,
(leaving the rest behind on their
Cushions, as the custom of the
Country required) till they brought
me into a fair Chamber, wherein
there was a large Couch, standing
on four Feet of Ebony, and covered with a rich Mantle of Silk,
quilted with Wool, on which
there seem'd Poppies to grow:
They pointed to the Couch, and
set the Tapers in Sockets of Silver,
which were purposely placed on
each side the Couch, and so left
me

me to my repofe, clofing the Door
after them.   No fooner was this
done, but the moft Fragrant fent
imaginable began to allure my
yielding Senfes to a retirement; it
proceeded from a Smoak of burnt
Spices and Perfumes, which I
fuppofe, the Maids, by fome Tube,
transfufed into my Chamber
through the hole of the Door.
I was thinking, what a rare fub-
ject that would prove for *Eucompfius*
to exercife his Poetry on; but indeed the Virtue of this fweet Fu-
migation was fo effectually fopori-
ferous, that I had no fooner lay'd
my felf on the Couch, and cover'd me with the Mantle, but
the irrefiftable Charms of *Somnus*
locked up my wearied Senfes in
the Cabinet of Reft.   And fo I
lay, till a knocking at my Door
awaked me with this Tetraftich.

Arife,

Arise, O Man, for what is Sleep
But Death's Effigies right ?
The Fates will once thy Vitals steep
In a more lasting Night.

At which serious and apt *Memento*, I saw the Tapers began to confess themselves useless at the approach of *Aurora*, and as seeming desirous to resign their Office to a brighter Luminary, they hid their dying Heads in the Sockets, and yet in their very snuffs, left an odoriferous Savour behind them. Then I arose, and having taken a turn or two in my Chamber, and view'd the delectable and costly furnishing thereof, the four former Maids came in, and beckning to me to follow, they reconducted me into the same Hall, where having left me, four others came in with *Eucompsus*, and so
every

every one in the order they fat at
Supper, was conducted in by four
Maids, till we were all met, and
then it was found, that all of us
had a like ceremony ufed in all
refpects.   But while we were de-
bating on the paft occafions, ap-
plauding their Magnificence and
Hofpitality , the Venerable *Dra-
mefco* came in, according to his
promife, and defiring us to fit
down on our Cufhions, he himfelf mounted on a Step of Ebony,
oppofite to the Ivory Bafis, and
made this following Difcourfe to
us.

*Friends and Brethren , firft of all ,
as* Englifh *Men , I bid you welcome ,
but as* Chriftians , *I embrace your
Society.   That Bafis of Ivory being
Confecrated to Holy Ufes, I never ftand on
it, unlefs while I am Praying or Prayfing
of God ; but this whereon now I am , is
the place where I ufually Difcourfe ,*
                                        and

and it is of this colour, to signifie,
that all other talk is as much below
that, as black is contrary to white.
But these things are obvious, and of
themselves explicable enough.   I suppose you may all wonder to hear me speak
so readily your Language, in so remote
a Country; but you must know, that
our Dramesco's, whom you call Priests,
are taught from their Infancy, all the
most known Languages of the world,
which for the most part, we in a pretty
manner attain to, notwithstanding the
brevity of our Lives, which never
exceeds forty Years; nay we count
twenty a sufficient Age, though many
attain to thirty; but forty, as I said
before, is the highest apex, to which
our Life can or did ever climb. And
yet, some among us, have been found
able in all the Sciences, and skill'd in
fifty four Languages; a thing, which
to the Europeans may seem incredible,
but as soon as they know our circum-
stances,.

stances, it will not prove *so* difficult to believe. For the Nature of our Climate, it is *so* providentially disposed, as if Heaven intended to compensate the deficience of our time in a more vigilant aptitude to Industry; for he that is most wearied with Labour among us, in the space of twenty four hours, requires but one three hours Sleep, by which only he is sufficiently invigorated and refreshed: Besides, we have the presence of the Sun two hours and an half sooner than any in Europe, and find him setting but an hour sooner, so that our day gains of them one whole hour and an half; moreover Nature has enriched this Soyl with a soveraign Plant called Anthypuum, the Berries whereof being made into a Drink, do refresh us as well as any Sleep, and save us the loss of time; so that though our Bodies are so inconsiderable, and our Years so few, yet our Life may be

E   justly

justly reckoned the longest and most
proper Life, because it is hardly ever,
and then but for a small time deprived
of its operations, by that silent un-
active Interregnum of Sleep. And
I remember to have heard of such a
Drink, among you of England, which
is called by that improper name of
Coffee; you count that a great help
to vigilancy, and so I grant it may be,
but I can assure you, it is made of a
Plant which is the bastard Plant to our
Anthypuum, and has scarce one
scruple of the Virtue which belongs to
ours. I suppose, it is the way of Heaven to bless each Soyl with those Fruits
which are most congruous and agreeable
to the disposition of the Inhabitants,
and most profitable and necessary for
the sustenance of the Country. Our
people are for the most part Husband-
men, Gardeners and Keepers of Cat-
tle; only two Hundred thousand of
the Commonalty are in especial employ'd

ploy'd in digging of Mines, which a-
bound here, and coyning the Gold and
Silver, though there are but 50000 of
them work at it yearly. Others make
it their Trade to work in all kinds of
Silk, to make Tapestry, and Quilted
Works, and to make Apparel for the
rest of the Nation. Others that are
of the Militia, are sent every Spring
to the Sea-side, to break the Eggs of the
young Cranes, and kill the old ones,
as many as they can. Thus, every one
is helpful to another; one sort manures
the Ground, another defends the
Country: Another Cloaths us, another Feeds us, and another helps us to
Barter for what we lack, by enriching
our Coffers: So that every one being
content with his Profession, and every
Profession being sufficiently gainful,
(because we are all Industrious, and
know not those luxurious wayes of
spending, which others practice)
those that have much have but enough,

and those that have little want
nothing. Now the desire of Riches
being unnatural to our Constitutions,
and the wayes of Deceiving being un-
known, while every one enjoys his own,
no body is in want, and our own Soyl yields
us as much as the whole world could.
Hence having no need to fall to base
practises, we are all exercised in our own
Vocations, and when we are Old we
leave the practice and gains of our Trade
to our Children, who, (as we wrought
before to maintain them) are now, by
the Law both of Nature and our Land,
forced to nourish us, which they do
most dutifully: But if any neglect it,
as I never yet could hear of more than
two, the Judges, that go about to look
to such things, bring them from their
Fathers House, and having caused
their Eyes to be pull'd out, and bran-
ding them with the Figure of a Viper
in their Fore-heads, they send them
forth, thus helpless, into the Fields,

and

and fo thofe who refufed to nourifh their Parents, are now uncaple of finding nourifhment for themfelves; but being hated and abhorred of all, who fee them fo ftigmatiz'd, they wander about, till they dye defervedly mife-rable. And here the Good Man having made a paufe, and looking ftedfaftly on me, I thought fitting to make fome reply; and thinking nothing could prove more accep-table, than if I fhould retaliate him, by a narration of our Cu-ftoms, I prepared to anfwer him in that kind, though I was a-fham'd to fee how thefe fmall ones exceeded us: But yet, becaufe I doubted whether he might not have attained to the knowledge of them, as well as of our Language, I firft chofe to ask him, whether he had ever yet been acquainted with our wayes of Government, or would defire to hear any News from us? To which, he thus returned. *About 2660 springs past, (for we commonly use that part of the Year in discourse, for the whole, it being the only memorable time for Action with us)* there came into our *Country an* Indian Brachman, *(for so their Wise Men are called)* the first Stranger that our Annals make mention of, called Meleligenes *of a comely Personage, tall and long-Visaged, his Eyes black and sharp-sighted, his Hair and Beard as white as Goats-Milk, his Complexion Sanguine; and in short, his Aspect such, as could allure Mens love, and enforce their respect.* He was no sooner seen by some of our Nation, but they received him as a God, adoring him and offering him Presents; but when the King of Gerania *(which is the Name of our Country)* heard of him, he came himself to do him Honour, and carrying him into the Temple of

Jupiter,

Jupiter, *who was then God of the Land, made there a fumptuous Feaft for him;* at which, *he having Eaten little, and Drunk lefs, came to the King,* and *fpake to this purpofe in the* Indian *Language, which was fcarcely then underftood by our Ancestours.* O King! *I am no God, nor Perfon that merit fuch Divine Honours, but a* Græcian *Born, and a Man that have Travailed moft parts of the known World, to encreafe Knowledge.* I *have been in* Ægypt, *and feen the Wifdom of their Priefts and Magicians:* I have been in Perfia, *and converfed with their* Magi. I *have noted the Holinefs and Religion of the* Jews, *and read the Poetical Writings of their Learned King* David; I *have alfo examined the skill of the* Chaldæans *in the Stars; but preferring the ftrict and temperate Life of the* Indian Gymnofophifts, I *have converfed with them above this*

E 4

ten

ten Years; so that now by my Speech, Habit, and Profession, I seem a Native of that Country. But of all the People I ever met with, none, as yet, have appeared to me to Live so irregularly as your People do, who though they are naturally well enclin'd to Hospitality and a sense of Religion, yet being destitute of a sufficient Lawgiver, they live among themselves more like Brutes than rational Creatures. In short, give me Authority, O King, and I shall so employ my skill in cultivating their Manners, by wholsome Laws, and in Moddelling your Government by good Policy, that you shall have cause to remember me for ever. At this saying, the King fell down before his Feet, and testifying his ready acceptance, committed all his Affairs to the Discretion of this Stranger; but would suffer him to reside no where, but in the Temple of Jupiter, *with the Priests of that* God,

rtly, *because he esteemed him*
Deity, and partly, because
beside in that Province was
h for the reception of such a
Here then he abode, and after
stituted all those Laws, where-
and is yet governed, he di-
for increase of Knowledge,
s, which he called Lescha's,
or the Dramæsco's *or Holy*
other for the Talcomummi,
call Lay-Men; *and added*
rence, that the Dramæsco's
bred there, and trained up
ir Child-hood, in all the
nguages, and after the at-
of them in the Mysteries of
y, Ethicks, Metaphysicks,
my, and Geometry, *only;*
the Talcomummi *should*
the most proper Dialect of the
Tongue, and in that find out
ts of Nature, studying Lo-
Mathematicks, Musick,
and

and Ethicks, *which comprehend all
the liberal Sciences; and to this intent*, *he left us Forty Volumns, every
one in a several Language*, *which he
ever bore with him*, *being light Rolls
of* Parchment; *one whereof, contained
the writings of* Moses, David, *and*
Solomon ; *adding, that they had been
Servants to the true God*, *and that
by their writings*, *he had perswaded
himself*, *how the Heathen Gods should
shortly be demolished*, *and the true
God manifesting himself to the world*,
should teach Men a way to serve him ;
in the mean time he left us in our
Lescha *this wonderful Prophecy :*

Χῖ πρῶ ηϛ, ρὐ ἔπιτα, τὸρ᾽ ἰαϛτπα ὀρθὸϛ ἰῶτα,
Σῖγμα-ῑῡ,ὁ ϛμικρὸϛ κὶ ἄλοϛ σῖγμα Σ.ΛΩΤΗ᾿Ρ.

Which I may thus *English* to you,
Six hundred first, one hundred then,
     And after ten ;
Six, seventy and two hundred more
     Will bring to you the S A V I O U R.
                                    He

*He said when this number of Years
was complete, which is 986, we should
understand the Prophecy: Now, which
is strange, those Letters in* Greek,
*which make this number, being joyned
together in that order he placed them,
do constitute the word* Xεισ⊙, Christ,
*who was Preached to us in that Year,
which this Prophecy foretold.* After
*this he ordered such Castles as these
to be made in such places, that may
most annoy the Cranes; and shew'd
us the Nature of three most useful
things, the one of the Tree which he
called* Geranophonon, *which signi-
fies a* Crane-killer; *for if a Crane
doth but touch it, it makes the Claws
or Bills, or any other part, that tou-
ches it, to fall off, and soon destroys
that enemy of ours: Then he show'd
us the use of an Herb called* Moly *by
us, but by him* Cynocephalea, *which
being beat to Powder and drank in
Wine, is a soveraign Remedy against
Witch-*

Witchcraft and Poison. But this most profitable *Antidote*, whose chief Virtue lies in its *Root*, is so deep and strongly radicated in the *Earth*, that we ought to use our utmost care in digging about it, for fear of breaking the *Root*. And lastly, he taught us the manner of making that *Drink*, which we use instead of *Sleep*, and therefore he called it Anthypuum. And having done all these things of love for us, in the space of eight or nine years, he told us he would depart now for Greece, and promised to mention us to the *World*, in the writings he intended to publish, which he said, should comprehend the Vigour of the *Body*, and strength of a wise *Mind*, as a means to eternize his *Name*, which, though first he said was Melesigenes, he afterwards acknowledged it to be Homer, *that is blind, because his Country-Men seeing him not overcome as others, by vain Pleasures, which* begin

begin at the Eyes, they counted him
as blind, and therefore, called him
Homer, never confidering, that the
quick eye of his Reafon and Virtue
had purpofely clofed the Eye of Concu-
pifcence, with which, as long as Men
fee, they themfelves are no better
than blind. But when our King heard
of his intended departure, after all
his Prayers, perfwafions, and promi-
fes proved ineffectual to ftay him, he
offered him many large Favours, which
when he refufed to accept, the King
begg'd of him to fay what he fhould do
for his fake, that had done fo much for
our Country. He only defired him to
do three things; firft, to Erect a Temple, bigger than that of Jupiter,
and Dedicate it τῷ ἐλδσομένῳ Θεῷ, to
the God that was to come, and to honour him with no Sacrifices, but of
continual Prayer and Praifes, and to
that end to inftitute a Quire with
Songs and Mufick, to Blefs and Mag-
nifie

nifie him ; Then he desired him to give
his mind to Hospitality ; and to that
purpose , to provide Two hundred
Chambers in every Castle , and to
furnish them after the manner you saw
your Lodgings furnished : And lastly ,
he desired him to transmit his Laws
to Posterity , and to choose out every
Year some of the gravest and justest
Talcomummi to expound the Law to
the People , and to select out of them
two Judges for every Province in his
Dominions of Gerania : First, for the
Province of Gadozalia (so called, from
that King Gadozal) where is the
chief City , and the largest Men of
all the Pygmies , who are also the
longest liv'd and best Learned. Se-
condly , for the Province of Homeria ,
which took name from that Gymno-
sophist , where the People delight
chiefly in Caverns and Cottages, built
of Mud , and adorned with Feathers
and whites of Eggs. Thirdly , for
                                    the

the *Province* of Calingi, *where the*
Pygmies *are the smallest of all,*
Marrying at five years of Age, and
not living beyond twelve ; who chiefly
feed on Fish, which they take from the
River Arbis, *that runs through their*
Province. *And lastly, for the Pro-*
vince of Elyſiana, *ſo called, for its*
wholeſome Air and pleaſant Situation.
All this the King Gadozal *promiſed*
and thereto Swore by his Scepter,
which was made of Wood, and plated
over with Gold. *And ſo that God-*
-like Man left our Country, and left
an Eternal Memory of his Acts with
us, which the grateful King ſtrove to
encreaſe ſeveral wayes ; as firſt, by
a golden Image, repreſenting Homer,
giving Laws to the Pygmies, *with*
this Motto, ——

Ἄνδρεσσι Πυγμαίοισι νόμον ἠ θεσμόν ἔθηκα.

To Pygmies *I their Laws did give,*
And Precepts made, by which they live.
More.

Moreover, *he Instituted an Order
of* Greek-Talcomummi ; *who are
only permitted*, *beside their Mother
Tongue*, *to Learn the* Greek, *both
Verse and Prose* , *which they were
much assisted in by several admirable
Poems of his*, (*which he Wrote for
them*) *chiefly three*, *his* Thesmo-
phoron , *which contained all his
Laws in Verse*; *a small one called*
Epicichlides ; *and his* Margites,
which, *it may be*, *have never come
to your Hands*, *because he left them
wholly here* , *except some few Frag-
ments of them*, *which he took with
him.* And this Greek *Order from
him are called to this day* Homeridæ.
But I forgot to tell you, *that in that
Temple*, *which he wish'd to be built
To the* God *that should come*, *there
was an* Adytum *called the* Proseu-
cha, *over which* Homer *left this
Distich to be wrote in golden Cha-
racters*, (*for we soon had learned*
to

to make Letters by his assistance.

Ὑιὲ Θεῦ, τὰ μὲν ἐσλὰ ᾐ Ἀχομένοις ᾐ ανευκτοις

Ἄμμι δίδυ, τὰ δὲ λυγρὰ ᾐ Ἀχομένων ἀπάλαλκε.

which I thus Englifh *for you, becaufe every one may underftand me,*

O Son of God, give us what thou feeft fit ,
   Whether we pray for it or no ;
But as for Evil , never give us it ,
   Though foolifhly we wifh it fo.

And thus, by this mans means, we have not only loft our Barbarifm, but arrived to a prety degree of Knowledge, and have a way to underftand the Language, Cuftoms, and Government of all Countries, efpecially fince thefe Indies *have been fo open; for the* Indians *learn of* Englifh *or* Dutch *Merchants the Affairs and Tranfactions of other Countries, and*
            F   *from*

from them the Brachmans *learn the same , and they, in memory of* Homer, *send to us every Year with writings of those Matters.*

Here he paused again , and *Eucompsus* being a great admirer of *Homer* , began to be altered in his Countenance, with a more than perhaps moderate Joy; which, I verily believe, came but little short of a rapture, and would have soon extemporized an Ode or so, had not the three young Squires come, who making very low Reverence to the *Dramæsco* , he went straight out of the Room , bowing to no Body ; for it is a Law to the Priests, never to bow their Bodies to any but God , as being above all others, by virtue of their Function ; likewise they are never to be seen in publick , unless standing, to put them in mind of the uprightness of their lives , and to make them
more

more watchful and diligent.   Soon
after, the Ancient Gentleman came
in, and gave order to bring in
our Breakfaſt-Dinner, (for it was
inſteed of both, and between the
time of both; they in that Country having but two Meals a day)
which was done after the former
manner, the *Dramaſco* ſtill begin-
ning and ending the Meal with
his Oriſons.   But after Dinner,
while ſome of us were reaſoning
on the abſence of *Pandeiſon* and the
four Servants, not being able to
imagin what was become of them,
we ſaw him come with them very
cheerfully into the Hall, appearing
as well and ſound as ever, which
put us into no ſmall admiration,
conſidering how late it was ſince
we left him in that miſerable plight.
But we ſoon heard him from his
own Mouth acknowledge the
wonderful skill of the *Talcomummi*

F 2   Phyſi-

Physicians, and their wholesome Provision, made for Wounded or Sick, so that they keep none under their Hands above a day or two; which great proficiency in that faculty, cannot be attained to by other People, because, no where else are found such good Simples, such Sanative Drinks, such learned Treatises, and rare Experiments, such exquisite Care and Diligence, and such moderate and wholsome Diet, and perhaps such faithful Physitians too. And then I understood by him, how, at our first entrance, he was taken by the two hindmost Gentlemen, riding on Rams, (it being unlawful for Sick Strangers to enter the Hall) and suddainly laid on a Chariot, drawn by six Hee-Goats, and carried to *Physician's-Lescha*, where his Servants attended him, and in that short time his Arm was

Set,

Set, and the rents of his Face clofed up to admiration ; nay, and his very Cloaths were fo neatly ranter-draw'd , that no man living could ever difcern they had been torn.   Which kind ufage made *Pandeifen* as obftinately now affirm them good Angels, as before he would make them appear to be Imps of Hell.   And indeed that fall made him afterward ftand the furer ; for where before he thought every Bufh a Murtherer, and every breath of Wind a flatt'ring Traytor, confidering now the ill confequences of fuch pufillanimous Cowardize, he bore himfelf for the future with a far more virile and couragious Refolvednefs.

But now the Ancient Gentleman fat down among us , and bad his three Sons to difcourfe with us, about what he had ordered ; when

F 3   the

the youngest of them placing himself near *Encompfus*, began this
relation : *Worthy Gentlemen, seeming your selves young and vigorous
Blades, and being, I doubt, not well
skill'd in Military affairs, you would
take it kindly, I presume, if we
should deliver unto you the true manner of our War with the Cranes, it
being impossible, that you should be
ignorant of our Antipathy.* To pre-
*vent therefore your modesty, according
to the General, my Fathers Orders,
I shall tell you the whole Story, that
when you talk of us to the* Europæans,
there may be no mistake. And first,
*you must know, my Father, whom you
see, is the tallest Man, the most Aged,
and has been the best experienced in
this whole Realm of* Gerania ; *when
he was twenty Years old, his first Wife,
my Elder Brothers Mother, dyed for
grief, that one of her Sons had been
slain by the Cranes in a fierce skirmish* ;
after

after that, the late King Pantalcus
requested him to Marry his Daughter,
which he condescended to (though he
came of a more Honourable race,
from King Porus his Dwarf) and then
he was created Generalissimo of all
the King's Forces, Lord Hospitaller of
Geranea, and his Governour of this
Castle; to which he no sooner came,
but in revenge of his Sons Death, and
for love of his late Wife, he invented
this most artificial Snare, which you
saw from the high Ground, on the Battlements of our Castle. For the Cranes
being the only causers of Famin in our
Land, by reason they are so numerous,
that they can devour the most plentiful
Harvest, both by eating the Seeds be-
fore-hand, and then picking the Ears
that remain: My Father, to deceive
them, hath caused Earth to be spread
over the Roof, and to be raised into
Furrows, which are purposely full of
Seeds, by which these Creatures,

F 4   (though

(*though very wise*) *being cheated,
when they think to fill themselves, and
prejudice us, not only lose those hopes,
but their Liberty and Lives, being
made a Prey to our anger.* So that,
*where other Lords of Castles are scarce
able to pay their Tribute of one hundred Cranes Heads yearly*, my Father,
*though he has an immunity from all
such Taxes, as being the Kings Brother, doth freely, by the help of this
Snare, present him with two thousand
Heads a Year.* Now, (*not to mention
my Fathers* Acts, *which are more
than any History can equal, in respect
of his stature*) *every Spring-time,
I and my two Brethren go mounted,
as you saw us, with those six Captains
of our Horse, and their Companies,
down to the Sea-side, where the Cranes
build; at the first bleating of our Goat-
Horses, all the old Cranes leave their
Nests, and in them their young ones,
and fly about us with great fury, for
they*

they are very senſible of our Hoſtile
intent ; then our Valour is moſt con-
ſpicuouſly ſignalized ; for as they will
ſometimes daringly come on the ground
and endeavour, with their ſtrength,
to puſh us beſide the Saddle, ſome of
us have been ſo bold to throw by our
Weapons, and ſetting our ſelves firm,
to catch hold of their long Necks,
notwithſtanding the many Wounds
of their ſharp Bills, and ſo wringing
their Heads from their Bodies, to put
them as Trophies under our Belt.
And thus my Father hath often ſaid,
that day his young Son was ſlain (for
being then but tender, yet venturous,
he ſeperated himſelf from the reſt, and
having transfixt nine of them through
with ſo many Darts, when all his Weapons were gone, he was diſmounted,
and wounded to the Heart, with one
of their long and ſharp Bills)
that day, I ſay, he hath ſaid, and all
men acknowledge, that to comfort his
Wife

Wife for that loss, he presented her
with five hundred Enemies Heads, and
three hundred dozen of their Eggs,
all taken and slain with his own hands
and my elder Brothers. And many
such encounters we have had and must
have every Spring-time; but for all
this, they are so numerous, that in
Seed-time they come in Shoals to spoil the
Husband-man's hopes, and our nourish-
ment; There we being both Horse and
Foot, stand ready with Darts, Slings,
and Staves, to assail them with all
our Vigour. They chiefly aim at the
Head and Face, but those places we
have guarded with an Helmet of that
fatal Wood Geranophonon; which,
whoever of them touch, are sure to
dye. Now, that these Creatures
may not seem so inconsiderable, besides
the advantage of Flying and equalling
us in Bulk, but far exceeding us
though mounted in highth; they are
very wise and strong, as may be ar-
gued

gued by that immense way they fly after
our Harvest, which they alwayes expect. When they begin their Airy
Voyage, they all agree together, and
rank themselves in the perfect form
of an Oxygonical Triangle, something like the Roman Wedge, the
acute Cuspe whereof not resisting, but
penetrating the Air, still widens
the Gap, and quite takes off the force
of the opposite Wind, which would
else scatter and disturb their March.
Their Flight is to the sight very lofty,
the King flying formost, whom they
elect: In the Reer they place by turns,
a certain number, who are to direct
and encourage them with their Voice,
and keep the rest all silent. At Night-
times they set a Sentinel, or a Corps
du guard, holding a Pebble in their
Claws, which being let loose in Sleep,
and so falling, rouzes them again to
the Watch, and makes them ashamed
of their supine negligence. In the
mean

mean time the rest sleep securely, hiding the Head under the Wing, and standing alternately on each Foot. Their King sees forward on the March, and fore-tells what he sees. We have some of them tamed in our great Tower of Ainodnol, and these will wantonly make rounds, Dancing very pleasantly, though irregularly. It is known to your Men, that when they would pass over the Sea, they wisely choose the Straights between two Promontories, which we call Creumethopson and Crambis; by which means, when weary, they rest themselves. Having pass'd half way, they cast the Pebbles from their Feet, and the Sand from their Mouth, when they have touch'd the Continent. Which Sand they took, that by their silence, they might escape the knowledge of those Eagles in their way, to whose fury their Loquacity would else have betrayed them. For these, and

many

many more of their Customs, they de-
serve to be reckoned a Flying Com-
mon-wealth; and some of our Poets
have feigned, that because Jupiter,
(who himself being a Pygmie, *used*
to ride on the Goat Amalthæa) *had*
been displeased at the former Pygmies *for their frequent immolation of*
Goats (which we now hold Sacred) he
therefore Metamorphosed them into
Cranes, who still will fight with our
Goats, and having formerly been
Husband-men, come now in such
throngs to require the Fruits of their
Ground, and to expell us the Country.
But, if you please, you may smile at the
fancy: I shall only add this, that from
Seed-time to Harvest, we fasten a
thin net-like work on stakes, over our
plow'd Ground, so high, that the
Cranes cannot come to the Corn, and
yet the Rain and Sun-shine is nothing
hindred thereby; on the sides of which
expanded sheets we drive close stakes
of

of Geranophonon, *which, if they endeavour to pass, it kills them. Ana so by our Valour and Wit we not only are Masters of our own Land, but transmit our Empire to the People of the Air, and without a tedious watch, may securely expect a full Harvest.*

And here the Ancient Gentleman lifting up his staff, gave his young Son a sign to leave off, which he readily obey'd, and only putting into *Eucompsus* his hand a Volumn, which contained his own History, he rose and left his place to be supply'd by his Brother; who was of a long Visage, straight Hair, Sanguine Complexion, grey Ey'd, and of a moist Palm. He being drawn near me, began this subsequent Discourse :

Gentlemen, you having heard the Original of our Laws, of our Wars and Customs, may further, I suppose, desire to understand after what manner

we

we expreſs our Love and Courtſhip to
the Female kind, the Intrigues of
Love not being the ſmalleſt part of a
young Man's enquiry. Firſt then,
(for I love to be brief in talk,) where
there is a lawful Affection, it can be
no where kept ſo inviolable as with us.
Our pretences are not long, but after
both parties are agreed, they muſt
have the conſent of their Parents,
(who ſeldome here dye before their Children are Married) which being ob-
tained, the next New-Moon they are
joyned, after which, they make a Feaſt,
Inviting all their Friends and Rela-
tions, who, after the Fathers and
Mothers of both have given their
donation, caſt every one, according to
their ability, a certain ſum into a
Box, provided on purpoſe, which ſerves
them for their Portion. So that Por-
tions among us are never regarded,
we being naturally more Generous than
your great Nations, and not thinking
fit

fit to esteem the Compartner of our
Lives by the Parents Dowry, but
rather, by what Nature and Virtue
hath made their own. As for that
filthy Merchandize of Bodies, which
you call prostitution or whoredome, we
are utterly unacquainted with it,
partly, because the Nature of our Women is more modest, partly, because
they have all a livelyhood with such
practices, and abhor to gain any thing
unlawfully; and partly, because we
have such an esteem of Marriage,
(which would seem vain, if other ways
were suffer'd) that we count it the
most honourable state of Life, and the
most dreadful to violate; and therefore none are desirous of it, but they
are free to enjoy it, there being no
great disparity of Faces or Fortunes
among us: We are all naturally health-
ful, all straight Bodied, all Honest
and Generous, all affable and Religi-
ous; and all obliged to profess the
same

same Trades as their Parents have
done, by which they attain more skill
and more riches. Only, if they have
many Sons beside the eldeft, fome are
bred up for the increafe of the Militia, fome for the Lefcha of the Talcomummi, (for the Prieft's Sons
fucceed them in the Dramæfco's Lefcha) whence they either practice
Phyfick or Law; or are Singers in the
Temples, or Secretaries of Learned
Men, or Councellors to the King,
and nothing is ever wanting to them
for the attainment of thefe things, for
the Lefcha's are maintained by the
Kings Charge, and every Science is
able to fuftain its followers. I might
tell you of our more Court-like way of
winning the Ladies Hearts, of their
Beauty, fweet Nature, Modefty, and
Affability; how filent, cleanly, indu-
ftrious and loving our Wives are; how
devout, fober, and grave our Ma-
trons; how lovely, ingenious, and

G   chaft

chaſt our Virgins; ſo that this three
hundred Years have given us no ex-
ample of any known Whore, dishoneſt
Wife, or immodeſt Widow: And ſo
indeed it is with the Men too; only
one Trebor Noſtaw, one of the
Talcomummi, was lately found
guilty of conveying away ſome Goods
and Monies from their Leſcha, and
decieving a faithful Friend, who
truſted in him; for which laſt Fact
chiefly, he was firſt diſgracefully expell'd the Leſcha, and afterward
ſtigmatized in the Forehead with
this Mark I. H. by which he being
known to have proved a falſe Friend, is
befriended by none, but caſt out, to
live as he can, or dye as he deſerves:
And ſuch puniſhments are the greateſt
we ever yet uſed in our Nation; becauſe there are ſo few Delinquents,
and becauſe the Shame and Miſery
may be more exemplary. But I cannot ſo ſoon paſs by Friendſhip, it being

a

a Virtue so honourable with us, and especially so pleasing to my self; and 'tis a common Proverb with us; Virtue and Friendship are the Twins of God. *At this time I have a Friend called* Mahdeen, *in the* Lescha *of* Dramæsco, *so sober and virtuous, so prudent and ingenious, so notable for his universal knowledge and remarkable Piety, that the hope and expectation of all pitch on him for the future ornament of our Church, and support of the Kingdome, by his Justice and Prudence; and notwithstanding our great distance, he sends me notice of his Affairs, and I commit all my concerns that lye that way, to his hands, not doubting of his Fidelity and Discretion.*

I remember a witty Distich he shew'd me on our new contracted Amity.

G 2 'Αυτὸς

'Αυτὶς μὲν χεῖρον εἶδ' ὅτι ἡμετέρη λάξεν
  ἀρχὴν
'Η φιλίη, αὐτὶς δὲ χεῖνϑ· ἐκ εἶδε
  τελωτὴν.   ;

I know the time, wherein our Love
  first mutually did bend ;
But Time Himself shall never prove
  so Wise, to know its end.

        which I requited with this,

'Ηέλιϑ σύ μοι ἴδι, σὺ μάξλυςϑ ἴδι
  σελήνη
'Ημετέρης φιλότηϑ. ἐπὶ πλέεν ὐ φανε-
  έσθω.

O Sun, thou glorious Prince of Day,
  And Moon, thou Queen of Night,
The Rays our Friendship shall display,
  Shall last as long as yours, and full as
                            (bright.

  The thoughts of this his friendship
and known constancy, are now the
chiefest solace I delight in, and his
                            memory

memory is the most pretious and gra-
phical Effigies of Virtue , that I can
bear about me: So that though such
an Affectionate Intimacy is here very
usual ; yet I dare affirm , that of
Mahdeen *and* Senrab (*which is my*
Name) to be the most defecated and
sincere.

And here again the Ancient Gentleman, lifting up his Staff, put
him in mind to conclude his Difcourfe, and give place to the Eldeſt
Brother, who fpake in this manner.

Worthy Sirs , having your minds
prepoſſeſſed with the knowledge of what
is moſt memorable with us, except
what I am going to tell you ; I think ,
your felves being put to it, could not
imagin any thing undeclared of more
importance , than Court matters. Of
them therefore I ſhall briefly inform
you. Our prefent Government (as it
was ever ſince we knew Civility)
Monarchical *, the moſt natural and*
beſt

best Government : But to omit the
Stories of our former Kings (which are
notable enough , but unfit for this time)
I shall only give you an account of
the present King.   You have heard ,
I suppose , by the Dramælco , that
our Kingdome of Gerania contains
but four Provinces, Gadozalia , Homeria , Caliægi , and Elyfiana ;
the Metropolis of Gadozalia is called
Ainodnol , the most large, rich , and
populous City of the whole Pygmean
Kingdom ; here our King keeps his
Court , here is the Centre of all the
Gentry and Nobility , and here flou-
rishes the practice of all Arts and
Sciences , which are highly esteemed
and cherished by the King , whose
Name is Sulorac , Son to Pantaleus
the late King , the manner of whose
Death was too Barbarous to be told to
any stranger , but the Actions and
Virtues of his life have already swoln
many Volumns.   He bears in his Coat
the

the Arms of each province quartered,
a Lyon paſſant in chief, an open Book,
whereon is written Θεσμοφὸϛοϝ, a Fiſh
and a Tree, the ſupporters are a Goat
and a Ram, the Horns Or, on the Creſt
a Cranes Head eraſed, and on that four
Crowns.   This King keeps the moſt
Royal Court of any Monarch, though
he maintains neither Life-guard, nor
armed Men, becauſe our Court is as
content and humble as the Country, and
the King himſelf hath proteſted he
fears nothing but Vice and Flattery.
In Apparel, I confeſs, they are almoſt
extravagant, becauſe they think Men
may lawfully deck themſelves with
what their own Country yields, if
they think themſelves not better than
others, becauſe finer.   But in Drink
and Amorous deſires they keep ſuch a
moderation, as if they were rather
Nymphs of Diana than Courtiers of
a King.   And this proceeds from a
virtuous reſtraint, not from a langui-

G 4   ſhing

shing impotency. So that they can practise
Love here, and please the Ladies, as
well as the most passionate European
Amoretto, but detest to abuse their
Bodies where the Scripture will not
permit. For Taxes, we are wholly
unacquainted with them, because our
King is never forced, like others, to
desire a supply, the Representatives
of the Nation, by the Peoples perswa-
sion, alwayes filling the Exchequer,
by their voluntary donations, not
doubting of the Wisdom of the King
and Councel, in disposing of it. But
yet, for the benefit of the Nation, it
hath been a custom of our Kings, to
impose on all the Governours of Castles
the Tribute of an Hundred Cranes
Heads yearly, which they duly pay
every Spring time. There are now
belonging to the Kings houshold, a Dra-
masco, a Poet, a Philosopher, a Physician, and a Painter, with whose
talk and works he is used to relax his
mind

*mind from the Cares of Empire.
He is a Juſt, Wiſe, Temperate, and
Valiant Prince, moſt generous in his
Largeſſes, and mild in his Puniſhments;
He ſends yearly to the Heads of each
Leſcha, to render him the Names
of thoſe, who are eminent in any
faculty, with their Age, ſtanding, and
behaviour; and as he ſees in his
Wiſdom, he provides for them rewards
according to their Deſerts, which muſt
needs be a great Encouragement to
young Learners. He hath lately, to
his eternal Renown, inſtituted an
Order called the* Royal Leſcha, *for
the increaſe and propagation of ex-
perimental Knowledge, by whoſe In-
duſtry, Philoſophy hath been more
promoted within this ten Years, than
in an hundred Years before. And
indeed, there is no ſuch progreſs made
in any parts of the World as here, in
Learning and Piety; for it is an
Epidemical Diſpoſition we all have,*
to

to shun our Labour, that will produce
Good, nor to embrace any Pleasure that
is Evil; because, if any Good thing
is done with Labour, the Labour soon
passes away, but the Good remains;
and if any Evil is done with Pleasure,
the Pleasure soon vanisheth, but the
Evil sticks behind.

And here he broke off, at the
sign his Father gave, and within
a while after, our Supper was
brought in after the former manner.
Only having understood that Eucompsus was a great admirer of
Homer, and not unhappy in *Greek*
Poetry, they brought in after Supper, a *Greek Talcomummi*, one of
the *Homerides*, who was lately
sent thither by the King, about
some business; when the youngest
Squire pointing to him, gave Eucompsus intimation of it, who thus
accosted the *Pygmie*:

Eucomp-

Eucompſus.

Ἄρχεο ἑλληνιστὶ λαλεῖν, τί τ᾽ ἐφίζομαι αὐτός·
Οὐ γὰρ ἀϊδρὶς πάμπαν Ὁμήρου ἐνθάδ᾽ ἱκάνω.

Pygmie.

Δὴ τίς τ᾽ ἐμοὶ τίς δ᾽ ἔνεπε, πόθεν τοι δῶμα πόλις τε;

Eucompſus.

Γραίη μοι πόζε δῶ. Λονδῖνον δ᾽ αὖτε πέλνα.

Pygmie

Οὔνομα σοὶ πῖον; τίω γὰρ φύσιν ἔνομα δείξει·

Eucompſus.

Εὐκομψόν με καλεῦσι πατὴρ καὶ πότνια μήτηρ.

Pygmie.

Ναίγε μοι Εὔκομψε νῦν φαίνεαι ὅζε Ὁμήρου,
Ἀνὰ φίλε Μέσησι, πόθεν μάθες ἔργα θαλάσσης;

Eucompſus.

Κλωθώ μοι τῆ πιν νῆσεν πόνον, ὄφρ᾽ ἀπὸ γαίης
Τηλόθι Βρεπτάδε πλαγχθεὶς καὶ ἀλώμενε αὔτως.
Πολλῶν ἀνθρώπων, νόον, ἄσεα, θεσμὸν ἴδωμαι.

Pygmie.

Πρῶ πιν μψ μοι Ὁμηρε, ἀτὰρ νῦν φαίνε ὁ δυασδ᾽ς·
Ἡμετέρους μψ γάρ τε νόμους μάθες ἠδὲ καὶ ἄλλων,
Ὄφρ᾽ Ἄγγλε περ ἐὼν νῶ Ἀγγελε ἀπονείαι·

Eucompſus.

Δὸς δέ μοι εἰρημένῳ, τί περ ἀνκτίον ἔξοχόν ὄζι;

Pygmie.

Ἔργα Θεοῦ πρῶπιν καὶ γείπνε ἠδὲ σεαυτῆ.

Eucompſus.

Εἰπὲ δέ μοι, πόσα ταῦτα τέλ᾽ ἔργμαλα ὄφρ᾽ ἂ εἰδῶ.

Pygmie.

Γράμμαλα ταῦτα λαβὼν σέο πιν᾽τ᾽ εἰδήσευ ἔργα.

which

Which short Dialogue is thus ren-dred in English.

Eucompsus.

Begin in Greek, *I'le answer you the same ,
For not in* Homer *rude I hither came.*

Pygmie.

Where was you Born ? Where did you after
(live ?

Eucompsus.

London *my Birth,* Cambridge *did Breeding
(give.*

Pygmie.

Tell me your Name ; Names oft the Nature
(show :

Eucompsus.

Eucompsus : *Both my Parents call me so.*

Pygmie.

That shows you're learn'd and witty, Nature
(right ;
But why, being learn'd, do you in Seas delight ?

Eucompsus

Clotho *this toyl ordain'd, that far from home,
A stranger I to other Lands should come ,
And view the Laws, Cities, and Minds of
(some.*

Pygmie.

Pygmie.

Homer at firft you feem'd, *Ulyffes* now ,
For our (and others) manners well you know
And at return your skill to friends will fhow.

Eucompfus

But tell me what all men fhould chiefly do ?

Pygmie.

Duties to God, themfelves, and Neighbours
(too.

Eucompfus.

But tell me, how many thefe Duties be ?

Pygmie.

Perufe this Volumn, and therein you'll fee.

And faying this, he gave him
a fair fmall Roll of Parchment in
very fmall Charaders of Gold ,
digefted into three Columns ,
which you fhall find Tranflated
out of the *Greek*, at the end of
this Narration ; and he added, how
every *Pygmie* Man and Woman
was from four Years old obliged to
read it over once a day, all their
Life long ; and to that end, bore
it alwayes about in their Bofom ,
excepting

excepting only that his Order had
them in *Greek*, and all the rest in
their Mother Tongue, which every Parent is bound to teach his
Children, not only to Speak, but to
Read perfectly. After all this, we
thanked the Ancient Gentleman
for all the knowledge imparted to
us, and kindnesses conferred on us,
promising, if ever we return'd
to our own Country, to publish
their Hospitality and Goodness;
and so we declared our stedfast purpose of leaving them the next
Morning: which when they perceived, they professed how loath
they were to part with us, and
promised all possible accommoda-
tions, and so taking our leave of
them that Night, we were conducted to our several Lodgings,
after the usual manner. The next
Morning early, the youngest of
the Brothers expected *Eutompsus*

at his Chamber Door, who was at that inftant confidering and devifing to fpeak with him before his departure ; fo that as their intent was mutual, their meeting found no impediment ; but after the tedious ceremonies of their obliging Difcourfe , the young Squire embraced *Eucompfus* his Knees, and he lifting him up in his Arms, kiffed his tender Cheeks, and promifed to extol the Virtue of that fmall People, but chiefly that of him, to all the greater Nations he fhould come to : And faying fo, he gave him a prety confiderable Volumn in *Greek*, which he had formerly compofed in his youthful days , with his lively Effigies on the Frontifpiece ; and the grateful *Pygmie*, in requital of fuch a worthy prefent, gave *Eucompfus* many precious and choife Rarities, among which there was

his

his own Picture, enchased with
Diamonds, drawn to the life, and
when unfolded, expressing his true
Stature, which *Eucompsus* received
with abundant testimony of his
joy and gratitude. But by this
time *Sol* had drove his Chariot almost half way towards his Noon-
baiting place, in a high Town
called *Meridies*, when the other
two Brothers having loaded me
and my other Friend with excel-
sive Complements and Presents, we
were at last dismissed with twelve
Chariots of Provision for our
Ship, drawn by Hee-Goats, who
went directly, without lash or
threat, before us, and the nine
Ram-Horse-men accompanied us,
as they had met us the other day,
to the utmost limit of the Mountain tops, and bidding us, after
we had taken out the Provision,
to send the Chariots back again,
they

they left us : But when we returned to the Ship, and had already
fpooned her for Launching, we
faw thofe well-taught Creatures to
go directly homeward in the fame
order they came loaded, but with
much more fpeed : And we all
admired at the Works of God, and
the power of Nature, who hath
made fo fmall a People fo Wife,
that they fail in nothing of that
abfolute Dominion our felves have
over the Creatures.

Χδεις βαιοῖσιν ὀπηδεῖ.

H   COLUMN

COLUMN I.

You that seek Life, Pleasures, or
  worldly store,
Seek God; He's Life, Joy, Riches,
  and much more.

First, love your Maker, let your mind
  Be chiefly to his wayes inclin'd;
Still seek his Glory, and proclaim
The sacred Honours of his Name.
And when perhaps you chance to read
His mystick Oracles, take heed
That no base mungrel thought divert
The understanding of your Heart;
Pull off sins veil, and put on Grace,
For God and you speak face to face:
Then with due reverence hear his
  Voice,
'Twill make your Soul and Bones re-
  joyce:

And

And what e're Law he shall impart
Write on the Tables of your Heart :
His Word is Life, his Word's a
   Treasure,
Beyond all Time, without all mea-
   sure.
When tow'rd his Temple you proceed ,
Repent of every evil deed ;
Request his Grace and special aid ,
That you may practice all that's said.
With Tears your Temple purge within :
God will not dwell in Hearts of
   Sin.
His Sacraments with meekness take ,
And for your precious Saviour's sake ,
Send forth a Sigh or two, and say ,
O Lord, who can thy Love display ?
Who thus didst Sin-kill'd Souls revive ,
And dy'dst thy self, that we might live ?
With such unfained thoughts desire
To praise Jehovah, *and lift higher*
Your Earth-clog'd Soul, that it may rise
Unto a pure Love-Sacrifice.
God doth no fragrant incense crave ,

Nor blood of Oxen would he have ;
He such oblations doth detest ;
A contrite heart affects him best.
An Heart Sin-loathing , sweetly
   Praying ,
And not unto the Tongue gain-
   saying.
Make not long Prayers for ostentation ;
Seek peace, if you expect Salvation ;
Christ was his Fathers Love, and
   he
Would have his Church alike to
   be ,
Knit as one Soul in Peace and Love ,
Receiving Pattern from above.
   Approve your self as one that bear
The Glorious Name of Christ, and are
An Heir to such a Kingdom's right ,
whose Glories are transcendant bright.
With cheerfulness desire still
You may perform your Maker's Will ,
Acknowledging all as his due :
Believe't ; He doth much more for you.

COLUMN II.

If farther you would lead a blame-
   lefs life,
Seek Virtue, love your Neighbour ,
   hate all ftrife.

HOnour the King ; and ftill obey
   Thofe, that do juftly bear the
   fway ;
Kings are Gods Images , and fo
(Next him) To them we duty owe.
Reverence thofe of high degree ;
Your equals love, and thofe that be
Inferiours , ftudy to defend :
'Tis hard to find a poor Mans
   Friend.
   The Embaffadours of Chrift efteem,
Follow their wayes ; but if they feem
In manners from Gods Word to ftray,
Hate what they do ; do what they fay.

H 3   Ho-

Honour your Parents, and at need
Their Bellies with your labour feed ;
Cherish the Poor , Honour the Old ,
All men with Charity behold.

Speak not unto your Neghbour fair
If hate within your heart you bear ;
Freely disclose what you intend ,
There's nothing worse than a false
Friend.

Think not that Man is truly Just
That's undefil'd with Theft or Lust ;
But he is so , who flies away
From Vice, and Sins not , though
he may.

If you desire to live and see
The comforts of Posteritie ,
Abstain from Sin ; 'tis that alone
Gives wings to Death , who else hath
none.

If God hath lent you worldly store ,
Stew'rd-like, distribute to the Poor ;
Who Sow in Love, will Reap in
Peace:
Thus scatter'd Seeds bring great
increase.   *Affect*

Affect your Neighbour ; and ex-
    press
Your Charity to th' Fatherless.
What in another Man you blame ,
Abhor your self to do the same.
To shun contempt, be grave, and bear
A look not proud, nor to austere.

Be as you seem , for time will bring
To the World's Knowledge, every thing.
In all Affairs few Words are best ;
Wise Men act most and prattle
    least.

Think not those powerful Men, that
    be
Subduers of an Enemie :
He's the best Conquerour , that knows
To pardon Crimes, and love his Foes.
That swayes the Passions of his mind ;
And serves not Vice in any kind ;
That is no slave to his desire ,
Nor burns in Lusts polluting fire ;
That knows to manage any state ,
And scorn the threats of slipp'ry Fate.

COLUMN III.

One Duty more, if you would
   perfect be,
Love your own self; cherish your
   Familie.

Honour you Bosom-Friend, and be
  Her shield against all Injurie;
Be not morose in taking wrong,
But put a Bridle to the Tongue;
'Tis a great Sin, for Man and wife
To spend their dayes in mutual strife;
For those, whose Bodies Heaven hath
  joyn'd,
To be so different in Mind.
No curse more sad than that; no state
More troublesome than such debate,
If she's good, why should he complain,
If bad; bad speeches are but vain.
Silence perhaps her will may force,
But Scolding sure will make her worse.
              Grant

Grant she be bad ; are you not so ?
If without Sin, the first stone throw.
But Husbands may perhaps offend ;
And Wives their Duty should attend.
Oh ! no, if Men bad actions do,
Well may the Women do so too.
If any Pain afflicts the Head ;
The whole's thereby endangered.
   Shun fiery wrath ; for wrath hath
     slain
Millions of Souls and wrought their
     bane.
Be Master of your Anger, and
Over your Pleasures, bear command.
   Hate chiefly bruitish Drunkenness,
Which makes, Purse, Life, and Credit
     less.
It is unfit Drunkards should be
In any sober companie ;
And for the Sober 'tis unfit ,
That they with Drunken Men should
     sit ;

                           Sad

Sad Men, who lose their Stamp
   Divine,
Changing their Shape to filthy
   Swine.

Talk not of what's a Sin to do;
Nor prove unto your word untrue.
Follow your Trade, and purchase Gold,
By youthful pains, against you're Old.
Some heap up riches many a year
To leave unto their Children dear;
But Riches quickly find a blast
When Virtue will for ever last.
If therefore Virtue you can give
Your Children, they've enough to live.
This is a Portion, which no fume
Of Sparkling flame can e're con-
*   sume;*
This is that Portion that will be
Their conduct to Eternitie.
Whatever thing in hand you take,
That you may it successful make,
Weigh it with due deliberation:
Nothing's more safe than consul-
   tation.

If Fortune on your actions Smiles,
Know, she first laughs, and then
   beguiles.
*Nay, though forever Wealth should
   stay,*
Death and Time hurry Men away.
Yet still endeavour in your mind
That a good Name you leave behind.
If Providence doth cast you down,
And angry Fates begin to frown;
Be patient, and this Maxim know,
There's nothing certain here be-
   low.
In all your actions take due care,
*And act, as if the King were
   there.*
*For the King's KING besure doth
   spie*
*Your Deeds; nay Thoughts, that dee-
   per lye.*
Use Moderation most of all;
For too much Honey's worse than
   Gall.

Think

Think on the shortness of your breath,
Think on our loving Saviours Death;
Let Heaven's Joys, the Worlds Tem-
  ptation,
And pains of Hell be still your Me-
  ditation.

To

To satisfie the Readers curiosity, I shall here produce the *Epitaph* of the *Pigmie* Governours Son, that was Slain in a Battle with the Cranes, mentioned *pag.* 73. as I afterwards Translated it out of the *Greek*.

The EPITAPH.

Parca hujus tenuem descerpsit forfice lanam

Et quæ vix potuit fila videre, scidit.

This Distich was writ in *Latin*, in the front of the *Epitaph*, at the end of which there was written in great Letters,

BAVHVS: ANTVERP.

JESUIT. EPIGR. LIB. II.

And then followed Ἔνθα Κεῖμαι, &c.

Thus

Thus rendred in *English*,

This Tomb doth hold
A Pygmie *bold;*
Who when alive
In Arms did thrive;
But a Crane's Bill
My life did spill;
And here I have
A fitting Grave.

If you ask why these Verses are so
short,
Attend and take this serious reason
for't;
I was but one foot long; these two,
you see;
Though short, they are one foot to long
for me.

FINIS.

An Advertisement of Books, Sold by Obadiah Blaygrave, *at the Sign of the* Printing-Press *in* Little-Britain, *over against the* Pump.

BLagraves *Supplement or Enlargement to Mr.* Nich. Culpeper's *English Physician*, containing a Description of the Form, Name, Place, Time, Cœlestial Government, and Virtues of all such Medicinal Plants as grow in *England*, and are omitted in his Book, called *The English Physician*, and supplying the additional Virtues of such Plants wherein he is defective. Also the Physical use of all Drugs which are brought from beyond the Seas, and sold in *Apothecaries* Shops. To which is added, a new Tract of *Chyrurgery*, for the Cure of Wounds made

The Perfect States-man, *or Mini-ster of State*, wherein are briefly set forth the true nature of the Subject, the endowment inherent to his Person, the method of his Election, Inftitution, and Recep-tion, the object of his Office, di-ftinguifhed under fuch Principles as are immediately requifite to the Eftablifhment of a Common-Welfare, by *Leonard Willan* Efquire, in *Folio*, price 5 s.

A Relation of a Journey of the Right Honourable my Lord *Henry Howard*, from *London* to *Vienna*, and thence to *Conftantinople*, by *John Burbury* Gent. in *Octavo*, price 1 s. 6d.

The Hiftory of Jewels, and of the principal Riches of the Eaft and Weft, taken from the Relation of divers of the moft famous Travellers of our Age, attended with fair Dif-coveries conducing to the know-ledge of the Univerfe and Trade.

The

The History of *Philip de Commi-nes* Knight, Lord of *Argenton*, with Annotations, in *Folio*.

Juvenal's 16 Satyrs, Translated into *English* by Sir *Robert Stapleton*, with Arguments and Marginal Notes, in *Folio*.

Mr. *Joseph Caryl* his large Commentary on *Job*, in twelve several Volumns, in *Quarto*,.

A Treatise of the nature of a Minister in all its Offices, To which is Annexed an Answer to Dr. *Forbes* concerning the necessity of Bishops to Ordain, which is an Answer to a Question proposed in these late unhappy Times, to the Author, *what is a Minister?* by *William Lacy*, Bishop of St. *Davids*, in *Quarto*.

The Divine Right and original of the Civill Magistrate from God, as it is drawn by the Apostle St. *Paul*, in these words, *There is no Power but of God, the Powers that be are ordained of*

God,

God, Illuftrated and Vindicated by *Edward Gee*.

The Young Man's Warning piece, in large *Twelves*.

The Brazen Serpent, or Gods grand defign, *viz*. Chrift's Exaltation for Man's Salvation, in his Believing on him; or the right way to Regeneration, by *J. Horn*, in *Quarto*.

The Effays or Counfels of Sir Francis Bacon, *Lord* Verulam, *Vifcount St*. Albans, with a Table of the Colours of Good and Evil, whereunto is added the Wifdom of the Ancients, enlarged by the Honourable Author himfelf, and now more exactly publifhed, in large *Octavo*.

Parfons Law, or *a View of Advowfons*, wherein is contained the Rights of the Patrons, Ordinaries, and Incumbents, to Advowfons of Churches and Benefices, with
Cure

Cure of Souls, and other Spiritual Promotions, Collected out of the whole Body of the Common Law, and some late Reports, by *William Hughes*, of *Grayes-Inn*, Esquire, whereunto is added an Appendix, containing the Heads of the several Statutes made in the Reigns of King *CHARLES* the First, and King *CHARLES* the Second, touching the same points, which was never before printed, in large *Octavo*.

The practices of the High Court of Chancery, with the nature of the several Offices belonging to that Court, and the Reports of many Cases, wherein Relief hath been there had, and where denyed.

Studii Legalis Ratio, or Directions for the Study of the Law, under these Heads, The Qualifications of the Study, The Nature of the Study, The Means of the Study,

The

The Method of the Study, The time and place of the Study: by *W. P.*

The Complaisant Companion, or new Jests, Witty Reparties, Bulls, Rhodomontados, and pleasant Novels, in large *Octavo*.

Gerhardi Meditationis, in *Twelves*.

Historiæ Romanæ Epitome, in 24°.

Alexander ab Alexandro, *notis Variorum*, in large *Octavo*.

Historiæ Augustæ Scriptores, *notis Variorum*, in two Volumns, large *Octavo*.

Moses and Aaron. Civil and Ecclesiastical Rites, used by the ancient *Hebrews*, observed, and a large opened, for the clearing o many obscure Texts throughou the whole Scripture.

Archæologiæ Atticæ libri Septem Seven Books of the Attick Anti quities, containing the description of the Cities, Glory, Government

Divi

Divifion of the People and Towns, within the *Athenian* Territories; their Religion, Superftition, Sacrifices, Account of their year, and a full relation of their Judicatories, by *Francis Rous*, Scholar of *Merton* Colledge in *Oxon*.

Romanæ Hiftoriæ Anthologia Recognita & Aucta, an *Englifh* Expofition of the *Roman* Antiquities, wherein many *Roman* and *Englifh* Officers are parallel'd, and divers obfcure Phrafes explained.

An Advertifement of a moft Excellent Water for Prefervation of the Eyes.

THere is fold by the faid *Obadiah Blagrave*, a Water of fuch an excellent Nature and operation for prefervation of the Eyes, that the Eyes being but wafhed therewith, once or twice a day, it not only takes away all hot Rheumes and Inflammations, but alfo helpeth the
Sight

[   ]

Sight in a most powerful manner; a Secret, which was used by a most Learned Bishop deceased, by the help of which Water, he could read without the use of Spectacles, at the Age of 90 years. It was now thought fit to be communicated to Scholars and Students, that they would make a tryal thereof. A Bottle of which will last a considerable time, and the price of a Bottle being but One Shilling, with Directions how to use it.

The Spirit of *Scurvy Grass*, prepared by Dr. *Charles Blagrave*, is also sold by the abovesaid *Obadiah*.

F I N I S.

www.ingramcontent.com/pod-product-compliance
Lightning Source LLC
Chambersburg PA
CBHW030620270326
41927CB00007B/1257